THE TREE & THE BIRD

To Braedn, my son,
who will soon spread his wings,
take flight, and travel far beyond the valley.

THE TREE & THE BIRD

JEFF N. PYLE

The Tree's Life

The Tree lived up high on a lonely hillside, above and apart from the dense forest that filled the wide valley floor below. In front of him and across the valley, the sun rose behind tall, rocky cliffs that towered high above the treetops. Far away to the right, but just within view, a small lake and bright green meadow were nestled deep in the valley floor. To the left, the valley spread wide and the trees faded into grassy fields in the distance. And far beyond the fields, white-capped mountains cut a jagged line into the smooth curve of the horizon.

Spring had finally arrived and the forest leaves had begun to unfurl, spreading a fresh rush of green across the valley. With the warmth of the spring sun, life once again began to emerge from the safe places hidden under cover of the forest.

Another beautiful day, thought The Tree.

The Tree's view from the hillside was beautiful and he could see deep into the valley. Many birds stopped by the hillside for the high view over the valley, but sadly, only rarely in The Tree's life had a pair of birds built a nest in his branches. He was just too far from the safety and abundance of the forest below for most who wished to raise a family.

The Tree was still hopeful for new life in his branches, but so far no baby chicks had yet been born on the hillside. Over time, The Tree had come to accept that this view over the valley, though beautiful, wide, and full of life below, was his alone.

The Tree On The Hillside

A Brand-New Life

It was now early morning and another pair of birds had just landed in The Tree's branches. Many stopped by the hillside to look over the valley for a nesting place or for their next destination. The Tree was always happy for visitors, and always greeted them with a smile.

"Hello! It is quite the day today, isn't it?" said The Tree.

"Hello. Yes, it is," they said quickly, seeming rather distracted as they hopped through the branches. After a short while, they stopped and talked amongst themselves, then turned and flew back down to the forest.

Another fine couple passing through, thought The Tree.

Only a few minutes later, The Tree was pleasantly surprised to see the same couple heading back up the hillside. But this time, their beaks were full of twigs and grass.

Once back in The Tree, the birds immediately and purposefully set themselves to building a nest on the biggest branch. They worked very hard through most of the day to finish their task while The Tree sat patiently and quietly. The Tree smiled to himself, happy to finally see a new nest in his branches.

The very next morning, The Tree caught a glimpse inside the nest and smiled brightly when he saw a single, tiny egg sitting all by itself right in the center of a soft bed of feathers.

"Oh! I see you have an egg in your nest," said The Tree. "Congratulations to you both!"

"Thank you very much!" said the birds with pride.

The Tree then looked thoughtfully at the egg. Even though no egg had hatched in his branches before, he was hopeful that this one tiny egg would survive.

The Egg In The Nest

Early spring passed quickly and quietly as the forest below grew thick with green and full of life. All the while, The Tree kept a patient watch over the valley, and a hopeful watch over the egg in the nest.

One especially beautiful morning, The Tree noticed the two birds standing on either side of the nest, closely watching the egg. The Tree turned his attention to the egg as well, and to his happy surprise, the chick inside had begun to wriggle and push against the shell. The three of them watched very intently with patience and hope as the chick slowly chipped its way free.

For this new life emerging in The Tree's branches, it seemed as if all the other happenings in the forest below had been shushed and told to wait.

Finally, the shell cracked and broke away, and there he was, a brand-new life: The Bird.

The Bird's parents gently cleared the broken shell from the nest, then looked at the new baby chick with love and said, "We will call you Peep."

"That is a wonderful name!" said The Tree, shaking his leaves with excitement to celebrate this new little life in the valley.

For the very first time in The Tree's long and lonely stay up on the hillside, a baby chick would grow up in his branches.

Suddenly, strong emotions flowed through The Tree, and he thought: *I will give you all the attention and protection I can provide up here on this lonely hillside. I can only be here as you need me, but that I will be!*

My Little Bird

Fresh from the shell, Peep was a scrawny little guy with no feathers and his eyes were closed to the world around him. But his eyes soon opened, his feathers filled in, and he grew very quickly.

Before you knew it, he was a hungry young bird, stretching his neck up high with his mouth wide open, calling for his next meal.

The Tree grew very attached to this first new life in his branches, far more than he had expected. He had been used to spending nearly all of his time gazing out across the valley, but now he found that most of his time was spent marveling at Peep's new experience of life.

Baby Peep

Peep soon became very curious about the world outside the nest. Though he wasn't yet talking very much, his parents began to teach him about The Tree: "All of this around you is The Tree. The Tree lives with you, and you live with The Tree. The Tree shelters you from the wind and the rain, gives you shade from the sun, and protects you while you are young. The Tree will teach you and guide you as you grow. The Tree is your home in the valley."

Peep had lots of time to think and to look around the branches and leaves of The Tree while his parents were away from the nest. And though he didn't yet fully understand what the lessons meant, Peep often thought about what his parents had told him about The Tree.

One sunny and quiet evening, Peep waited patiently while his parents were out gathering food. He sat comfortably in the nest, preening his feathers and stretching out his growing wings. He was just getting ready to take a little nap when he found himself gazing at the leaves and branches surrounding him. Again, he thought of what his parents had told him, about how The Tree was here with him, and that he was with The Tree.

A new idea suddenly popped into Peep's mind, *what if all of this IS The Tree?* Then he wondered further, *if I said something, would The Tree answer?*

After some more thinking and another long, slow look through the branches, Peep decided to simply, but bravely, call out to The Tree: "...hello?"

The Tree had been eagerly waiting for this moment and let out a quiet chuckle. Then softly, he said, "Hello, my little bird. It is good to meet you."

Peep's eyes grew wide and he sat very still for a moment, surprised to hear The Tree actually answer. Then he sat up a little taller, and with a bit of lingering uncertainty, answered back, "Hello... I mean... I've heard a lot about you, that you are my home and you will take care of me. I'm happy in my nest, and I like my home."

"I am very glad to hear it," replied The Tree with a smile. "I have kept watch over you, and have done my best to keep you protected in my branches."

"Thank you! I do feel safe here," said Peep.

"That is also good to hear," said The Tree. Then he added, "I see your feathers have grown and you have begun to exercise your wings."

"Yes! My wings are getting really big! I can pick myself up off the nest with one flap!"

With a chuckle, The Tree answered, "That is great, my little bird. I think you will be a wonderful flyer one day."

"Yeah, I will!" Peep said proudly.

The Tree stood up tall and lightly shook his leaves with new pride. Having shared these first few words with the new little bird in his branches, he was happy as one could possibly be.

Peep and The Tree continued chatting cheerfully with each other until Peep's parents returned. Peep was fed and tucked into bed, and then, for the very first time, The Tree and Peep said goodnight to each other.

A Little Walk

The next morning was bright and clear with little rays of sunlight passing through the leaves. Peep's parents had left for the forest to eat their breakfast and to gather up a meal for Peep.

The Tree looked at Peep through the stillness and asked, "How would you like to go on a little adventure today?"

"What do you mean?" Peep replied casually, slightly distracted with preening his feathers.

"We talked before about being a good flyer, but the first step to becoming a good flyer is to take a walk along the big branch." Then The Tree asked, "Have you been out of the nest, yet?" Though The Tree knew very well that he hadn't.

Peep stopped preening rather suddenly and took a timid look over the edge of the nest to the big branch. He followed the branch slowly and steadily with his eyes as it stretched far away to the leaves of The Tree.

"Well... not really," Peep said. "I've been on the edge of the nest to flap my wings, though."

"The big branch is very strong, my little bird. You do not need to worry," The Tree reassured.

"I'm not worried, but..." said Peep with reservation, staring even more intently at the branch.

The Tree stayed quiet for a moment to give Peep some time to think, then said in a soft voice, "I am here for you."

The Tree's reassurance seemed to calm Peep a little. So, still looking intently at the branch, Peep slowly stepped up onto the edge of the nest. He focused on a spot right in front of him and shuffled his feet back and forth a couple times.

The Tree gave an encouraging smile as Peep bravely faced the new step he was about to take.

Finally, Peep leaned forward, spread his wings about halfway to balance himself and hopped off the edge of the nest and onto the branch.

After a small moment of quiet triumph to himself, Peep looked up at The Tree with a big grin across his face.

The Tree's smile grew wider and he rustled his leaves to celebrate. "Very good, my little bird!"

Peep again looked down the length of the branch and started slowly walking away from the nest. About halfway down the branch, he stopped to look back. For the very first time, he saw the nest from the outside. He even saw new branches on the other side of The Tree that he couldn't see before. It felt like he was in a whole new world.

Peep then started walking back toward the nest, but this time a little faster and with a little more confidence. He even hopped a few times with his wings slightly spread out.

When he got back to the nest, he looked into it thoughtfully, but only for a split second. He then turned right back around and hopped faster and faster down the branch. He spread his wings out a little bit more, making longer and longer hops, even gliding some of the way. In no time at all, he had made it all the way to the end of the branch and was headed back toward the nest.

Peep continued joyfully hoping and gliding, back and forth down the big branch while The Tree brimmed with joy at how well Peep had embraced his very first adventure.

Watching Peep master the big branch so quickly, it was obvious to The Tree that Peep could tackle even bigger adventures. "You were born on my biggest branch, little Peep, but there are many other branches for you to explore," said The Tree. "You could surely hop to the one right next to you pretty easily, I think."

Peep stopped all at once and turned to look at the branch. Suddenly feeling nervous again, he said, "I don't know if I can jump that far."

"Oh? But you were just gliding very nicely down the big branch. Maybe you can do the same to glide across."

Peep slowly looked over the edge of the big branch and down to the ground below. He then looked back up at the branch in front of him and said, very plainly, "It looks a little scary."

With a calming voice, The Tree said to him, "Most new things seem scary at first, my little bird. You do not have to do it right now if you are not ready."

Peep stayed quiet for a moment and took another long look over the edge. Finally, he looked back up at the branch in front of him and said to himself, "It won't be scary all the time."

He then stood up tall to build his strength and took a quick, deep breath. Then, without much more warning, he leaned forward and spread his wings.

Pushing off with his feet, he gave a light flap and glided gracefully toward the other branch. He reached out with his feet, gave another light flap to slow himself down and landed gently and perfectly.

Peep was still staring at the spot where he landed when, very calmly, he said, "I did it."

"That was wonderful!" said The Tree, surprised at how quickly it happened, "I am very proud of you!"

Peep On A New Branch

Peep immediately looked ahead to another branch. Without hesitation, he glided gracefully across, and then to another. Before he had time to even think about it, he had gone all the way around The Tree and was right back by the nest. Peep looked up at The Tree with pride and gratitude and said, simply, "Thank you."

"Thank me?" said The Tree, a little surprised. "You did it all by yourself, and it was very wonderful to see!"

"Yeah, but you made it easier," said Peep.

"Well, you are welcome," said The Tree humbly. "I am here for you, my little bird."

All By Myself

Peep spent the next few days happily hopping and swooping through the branches of The Tree. Around and around he would go, so full of excitement that he couldn't help but let out little squeaks of joy along the way.

Sharing in Peep's excitement, The Tree said, "I could see you clearly the first couple of times around, then you became a blur in the air!" To which, Peep giggled with pride and went even faster around The Tree.

As Peep buzzed through the branches, he passed by a tasty-looking bug here and there. He was used to waiting for meals from his parents, but they had been spending more and more time away from The Tree and he had been feeling hungrier and hungrier the more he hopped through the branches.

After circling The Tree a few more times, another pang of hunger rumbled in his belly and he thought, *maybe I could catch a bug or two for myself.*

Peep quickly hopped to a branch with a bug on it and watched for a moment as it slowly crawled along. Then, very purposefully, he hopped over to it and quickly snatched it up with his beak.

Satisfied with his first catch, he smiled and thought, *I can do this on my own!* A new sense of independence rushed through him as he bounced happily through the branches, plucking up enough tasty bugs to completely fill his belly.

The Tree watched with pride as Peep happily gathered up his meal. *Growing up so fast*, thought The Tree. Then quite unexpectedly, an almost nervous thought crossed The Tree's mind, *Very soon, he will be grown up enough to fly out on his own...*

Peep was quickly growing more confident and learning his independence, and The Tree was grateful. But he also knew it meant that the time for spending all of their days together was nearing its end.

The Tree let out a long, slow sigh, then looked lovingly at Peep and said, "You are getting very good at taking care of yourself, my little bird."

"Thank you! I am!" said Peep proudly, still hopping through the branches.

"It is good to see," said The Tree softly.

Peep's parents had already returned from the forest and were watching from the top branches of The Tree. They had seen Peep gather his own food and came down to greet him.

"Hello, little Peep," they said. "We just saw you get your own food! We're very happy for you!"

Peep stood up a little taller and said, "Thank you!"

"You have grown up very fast," they said. "And now that you're able to get your own food, we've done as much for you as we can. And so, it's time for us to leave the hillside." Then, glancing toward The Tree, they added, "The Tree is a very good teacher. The Tree is your home, and he will guide you."

Humbly, The Tree answered, "He is a very courageous and adventurous bird, and I am very proud of him." To which, Peep fluffed up his feathers and smiled brightly.

The parents then looked at Peep with love and said, "Goodbye, little Peep. I'm sure we will see each other again in the valley."

"Thank you for feeding me and taking care of me," said Peep.

"You are very welcome," they said softly. Then, with another look of thanks to The Tree, they flew down to the forest.

Starting To See

At first light of the next day, Peep went right back to hopping happily through the branches of The Tree.

The Tree had grown to love Peep's constant company and was very content watching him grow up in his branches. However, he knew Peep needed to explore the valley and find his own way in the world, and he wanted to spark Peep's curiosity for more adventure.

So, The Tree said to Peep, "You have looked through the leaves at the end of my branches many times, my little bird."

"Yeah, I like to look out in different places to see different parts of the valley," Peep answered. "Also, there are more bugs by the leaves."

"Yes, that is probably true," agreed The Tree. "Could you share with me what you see through the leaves?"

Peep fluttered excitedly, happy to share his discoveries with The Tree. He quickly glided to the right side of The Tree and said, "Over here, it looks like there's some water down in the valley, but it's really far away."

"Yes, I think there is a small lake down there," said The Tree. "And yes, it is very far away. Though it does look like it should be a pretty place to visit."

Peep looked deep into the forest below them, then said in a more thoughtful voice, "It looks like it would be easy to get lost out there."

"The forest in the valley is very big, my little bird, but you should not worry about getting lost. Whenever you need to find your way, just fly to the top of a tall tree and look for me on the hillside. I will be here for you." To which, Peep smiled and was comforted by the thought.

Peep then hopped to the front of The Tree and said, "Out here, I can see all the way across, and there are big cliffs on the other side. It looks far away too, but not as far as the lake."

"The cliffs are very tall," said The Tree. "I do not even know what is beyond them. But, I think your wings will carry you over those cliffs someday."

Peep's eyes grew wide, he hadn't imagined yet what could lie beyond the edge of the valley.

Looking Through The Leaves

Then finally, Peep hopped to the left side of The Tree. "Over here, the valley spreads out really wide and seems to go on forever. As far out as I can see, there are some tall hills with white on top."

"There," said The Tree, "the forest ends and turns into grassy fields. Those hills in the distance are mountains and they are very tall, I think. Tall enough to hold the snow throughout the year. I do not know much more than that, but I think it would be a great adventure for you to see them up close. What do you think?"

"It would," said Peep, lost in wonder. "Are there any trees by the mountains?"

"Well, I think there should be a forest there, too," said The Tree, "but the only way to be sure would be to go and see for yourself."

With those words, Peep drifted into a daydream about flying to the mountains. For the very first time, Peep had real thoughts of adventures far away from the hillside. But, at least for today, Peep knew his world still lay within the branches of The Tree.

After gazing at the mountains a short while longer, he lazily and quietly made his way back to the nest and snuggled himself comfortably inside. The dream of an adventure to the mountains still swirled in his thoughts.

The very next morning, Peep was again full of energy and happily zipped around and around the branches.

"You are wearing little pathways all around me!" The Tree chuckled.

Peep giggled with excitement and went faster and faster until he finally stopped for a rest.

Taking the opportunity of the short break, The Tree said, "You have made all of these paths in a circle around me, but I wonder, have you ever thought of how the valley might look from the very top branch?"

Peep looked straight up through The Tree and suddenly wondered why he hadn't thought of that before. Then he said, "I guess it's not really that far up there, is it?"

"No, not too far at all," answered The Tree, "and I bet you could see the mountains much better from up there, too."

Peep perked up at the thought, and without hesitation, eagerly hopped and jumped his way upward. When he got to the top branch, he stood proudly above The Tree.

For the very first time, Peep was no longer within the leaves of his home. Before him lay the whole valley, all at once. It was as if he had discovered a new and giant kingdom, and he gazed deeply in silence for a very long time.

Finally thinking to look down, he said to The Tree with true wonder and amazement, "I can see everything from up here!"

Stretching Your Wings

Through the leaves, Peep's views of the valley had felt only like pictures of something to see, but now it felt so much more real. And from that, he felt new desires for flying out over the treetops and of adventures in the valley.

The Tree could see the changes in Peep's heart, and he knew that Peep's wings were meant for much more than just gliding through his branches.

As Peep was busy catching bugs for lunch, The Tree said to him, "It seems you have cleared nearly every bug from my branches. I wonder if you would find more at the edge of the forest."

Peep hopped to the front of The Tree, looked through the leaves and said, "I *have* been feeling a little hungrier lately."

The Tree paused for a moment, then added, "It would be your first trip outside our home, my little bird, but a good adventure to stretch your wings, I think. I am sure you could make it there and back pretty easily."

Peep had many thoughts of flying over the valley, but now that it seemed the time had come for him to leave The Tree, he again felt a little unsure of himself.

The Tree sensed Peep's hesitation, so he said very softly and plainly, "I think it is time for you to try."

From the certainty of The Tree's words, Peep felt a small bit of nervousness run through his body. It wasn't quite fear, but just that little anxious feeling you get when you're about to try something new.

"Remember, my little bird," reassured The Tree, "I am here for you."

"I know," said Peep softly, still looking down at the forest edge.

Peep took a long, deep breath, then looked for an open branch straight down from The Tree. *It won't be scary all the time*, he thought. He shuffled his feet back and forth a few times to build up his courage and took another deep breath to get ready for his first real flight. Then finally, he spread his wings and jumped out through the leaves.

Peep smiled when he felt the open wind under his wings as he glided gracefully through the air and down the open hillside. When he got close to the forest edge, he slowed himself down, reached out with his feet, and landed perfectly and gently on the branch below.

Peep had flown out of his home for the very first time.

Though it was a short flight, Peep felt very free and proud of himself. He turned to look up at The Tree and saw him proudly smiling back.

Peep suddenly realized that he had never seen The Tree from the outside before. Honestly, he hadn't yet imagined seeing The Tree from anywhere but within his branches.

The Tree was very big, much bigger than Peep had thought. With wide branches and lots of bushy leaves, The Tree stood alone and strong, high up on the hillside.

Peep felt very proud of his home in a way he hadn't before, and he instantly knew there could be no other tree like it.

The Tree also felt very proud as he watched Peep fly out on his own. Peep had grown up, and he was confident in himself. *My little bird,* thought The Tree.

Peep explored the new trees along the forest edge. He quickly noticed that there were definitely a lot more bugs down here. And with so many of them crawling around, and such a hungry feeling in his stomach, he ate maybe a few too many and filled his belly very quickly.

After another long bit of exploring through the trees, Peep stopped to take a look through the forest. *There are a lot of nice trees down here,* he thought, *but they are not my tree.*

Suddenly, he felt very eager to get back to his home. Without hesitation, he left the forest and flew quickly up the hillside. But, instead of flying to the branch he left from, he decided to dive down under The Tree's leaves and swoop up onto the big branch.

As soon as he landed, Peep announced very cheerfully, "I'm back!"

"Welcome home, my little bird!" said The Tree with a big smile. "That was quite an entrance!"

Peep felt very proud of himself and fluttered his wings. Then he said, "I like our home up here!"

"Thank you! So do I!" said The Tree. "And how did it feel to stretch your wings?"

"It felt really great!" said Peep. "It wasn't hard to get there, or to get back. It didn't take very long, either."

"That is good," said The Tree with a chuckle. "Imagine just how far you will go on those wings of yours. In fact, I think someday very soon you will fly over the whole valley."

A Little Farther

Peep woke early the next day and chimed a cheerful, "Good morning!" to The Tree.

With a slightly groggy voice, The Tree slowly answered, "Good morning, my little bird... You seem very excited today. Do you have something planned?"

"I do!" said Peep. "I'm going to explore the forest some more."

"Oh, I see! That does sound like a good idea!" said The Tree, very impressed that Peep had made such a big decision on his own.

Then Peep said very purposefully, "I'm ready to stretch my wings a little more!"

"That is good to hear, and I do think you are ready," answered The Tree. "I will be here for you when you get back."

Flying Over The Valley

Peep quickly hopped his way to the top branch of The Tree, then immediately spread his wings and set out on his first true adventure.

As he explored the forest below the hillside, Peep regularly stopped on high branches to check that he could still see The Tree. But as his confidence and excitement for the adventure grew, he began to dive deeper into the thick of the forest, sometimes popping up somewhere completely different than where he went in. Back and forth he went, crisscrossing the valley below the hillside, bobbing in and out of the treetops.

Out in the open valley, Peep saw lots of other birds flying through the forest and he said hello to many of them as he passed. They said their hellos in return with a smile, but Peep was so excited about his adventure that he never stopped in one place for too long.

Finally, after a long day of exploring, it was time for Peep to head back home to The Tree. He was in very good spirits and carried a new air of pride, and the feeling of a new-found connection to the forest.

About halfway back to The Tree, Peep let out a little call, *Te-Tee!* He had never let out a call like that before, but he was excited to share his adventure with The Tree and couldn't help himself.

When he was almost to The Tree, he let out his call again, *Te-Tee!* Peep then dove down below the leaves and swooped up onto the big branch. "Hi there!" he said, unable to hide the grin on his face.

"Hi there to you!" said The Tree. "And how was your adventure today?"

"It was great! I flew around the whole hillside. I kept going farther and farther and I could see the cliffs and the lake and the mountains up close... well, closer."

"That *is* a good adventure," said The Tree. "It was wonderful to see you flying out on your own!" Then more softly, he added, "I am also glad you are back."

"It was pretty amazing, that's for sure," said Peep. "I didn't really plan to go too far this time, but I could still see you and I kept wanting to see more of the forest. I'm excited to go out again tomorrow."

"I think you should," said The Tree, genuinely happy for Peep's excitement. "Your wings will take you anywhere you want to go, my little bird. And no matter how far your adventures do take you, I am here for you."

"I know you are, and I'm glad," said Peep.

Beyond The Hillside

Every day since his first journey to explore the forest, Peep steadily ventured farther and farther into the valley. He didn't need to look for The Tree nearly as often, and when he did, Peep usually knew right where he was. He felt like he was becoming very much a part of the valley.

Whenever Peep returned from one of his adventures, he let out his call, *Te-Tee!*, then swooped up from under the leaves and onto the big branch. Peep's call became his happy signal to let The Tree know he was heading home and had finished with his adventures for the day.

Whenever The Tree heard Peep's call ring through the air, he shook his leaves and lightly swayed his branches in true joy for his little bird's return. And with Peep back in his branches, The Tree listened eagerly, and usually late into the evening, as Peep shared his stories of what he had seen in the forest.

Early one sunny morning after gathering a good breakfast, Peep stood up tall and said in a very decisive way, "I'm going to fly to the lake today."

The Tree raised his eyebrows with a happy look of surprise and said, "Now *that* sounds like a grand adventure!"

"I'd like to see it up close," Peep continued, very much in control of his decision, "and today feels like a good day for a long trip."

"It is as good a day as any!" said The Tree in agreement. "I imagine you will have some very interesting stories to tell me when you return."

Then The Tree furrowed his brow and said, "You know, I cannot see around the hills to the right and I have always wondered about the stream which leads to the lake and where it comes from. Maybe you could find out for me?"

"Yes, I'll do that!" exclaimed Peep proudly, happy to solve a mystery for The Tree.

Peep would soon be very far away from the hillside, and The Tree showed the first sign of worry for his little bird. "I think it will take you more than one day to make it to the lake and back."

Peep noticed The Tree's concern, so softly, he said, "Yes, I think it will. But I'll be ok." This time it was Peep's turn to reassure The Tree.

The Tree sighed lightly and said, "I am sure you will." Then, managing a small smile, he added, "Be safe on your journey, my little bird. I am here for you."

"Thank you," Peep answered.

Peep then quickly hopped up to the top branch and looked back down at The Tree. He gave The Tree another warm smile of reassurance, then turned toward the lake and spread his wings.

The Tree watched thoughtfully after Peep until long after he had disappeared in the distance. Eventually, he slowly turned his eyes back to the wide view of the valley before him and let out a long, slow sigh.

Finding A Friend

Peep kept his eyes and mind focused on getting to the lake, and except for the occasional stop for a short rest and a snack, he traveled a long way in a fairly short amount of time.

On one of his rests, Peep looked back toward the hillside, which was now almost out of sight. He thought about The Tree and wished he could let The Tree know he was alright. But he knew The Tree would encourage him to finish his journey and say, "*It is ok, my little bird, I am here for you.*"

The thought of The Tree's support gave Peep renewed confidence. So he took a deep breath, turned back toward the lake and set off again.

After another long flight, Peep perched himself on a tall tree to have a look around. He was now most of the way to the lake and feeling a little tired. At the edge of the valley to the right, he saw a small waterfall tumbling gracefully from a short cliff to a misty pool below.

That looks like a nice place to rest, Peep thought. The waterfall was very inviting, and it wasn't too far off his path to the lake, so Peep made his way to the top of the cliff and landed on a rock at the edge of the fall.

Through the mist below, Peep noticed a gentle stream meandering through the grassy meadows. It stretched all the way from the pool to the lake in the distance. He smiled at his little discovery, happy to finally solve the mystery for The Tree.

The water crashing over the falls made deep rumbling sounds. Mist billowed up from the pool of churning water below and the sunshine from behind him painted glimmering rainbows in the mist. Between the deep song of the falls and the amazing view in front of him, Peep soon felt the weight of his long flight. His eyes became very heavy, and he felt very tired.

Resting At The Waterfall

Mesmerized by the sounds and beautiful scenery of the falls, several minutes passed by unnoticed as Peep drifted into dreamy, restful thoughts.

Then, very unexpectedly... "Hello!" rang a voice from just behind him. It startled Peep so much that he jumped straight into the air and had to flap his wings to keep himself balanced.

Peep quickly turned to see where the voice had come from. Standing on a rock just a hop away was another bird about the same age as him with a very amused smile on his face.

Peep stared wide-eyed at the other bird for a moment, then shook his head to clear his thoughts and said, "Uh... Hello!"

"I didn't mean to startle you," said the other bird, giggling a little. "I just saw you sitting here and I thought I'd stop to say 'hello'. My name is Cheep!"

Still recovering a bit, Peep said, "Oh... that's ok."

Cheep then said, "It's good to meet you, uh... what is your name?"

"My name is Peep," he answered, finally coming around.

Cheep looked curiously at Peep for a moment, then cocked his head and said, "We can be Peep and Cheep!"

"Yeah... yeah, that sounds good!" said Peep, perking up a little. The Tree always called him *my little bird,* and he realized that he hadn't heard his name out loud for a very long time. Then Peep added, "It's good to meet you, too!"

"Do you want to go explore the lake together?" offered Cheep. "I know my way around it really well."

"Yeah! Actually, that's where I'm headed." Peep was surprised at how nice it felt to have a friend to share the adventure. "Thanks for stopping to say hi."

"I'm glad I did," said Cheep.

The two new friends then happily set off toward the lake.

Home And Away

Back on the hillside, The Tree was very still and quiet. He had almost forgotten what it was like to be alone on the edge of the valley. And without Peep's company, the time passed very slowly.

He had invented a little hope that Peep would make it back from the lake before nightfall, but it was nearly evening and The Tree now accepted that he wouldn't.

It is ok, The Tree thought with a sigh, *my little bird is having a good adventure. I should not worry about him.*

But The Tree knew very well that he would worry anyway.

The following day passed just as slowly and it was now late in the afternoon. Just as The Tree had again begun to wonder how Peep was doing on his journey, a distant *Te-Tee!* floated through the breeze across the valley.

The Tree stood up straight when he heard the call and quickly looked toward the lake. Only a few moments later, and much closer, another *Te-Tee!*

The Tree finally caught a glimpse of Peep as he cleared the forest trees and began to swoop down under his leaves.

Landing lightly on the big branch right next to the nest, Peep fluttered his wings happily and gave The Tree a very cheerful "I'm back!"

The Tree could barely contain his joy at Peep's return and swayed his branches back and forth in excitement. "I was just thinking about you," he said.

"I thought about you, too," said Peep. Then he quickly added, "The lake is a lot farther away than I thought. It took almost the whole day just to get there."

"That is ok, my little bird, I understand," offered The Tree.

Then very excitedly, Peep said, "But I made a new friend! We met at a waterfall by the lake. His name is Cheep. He showed me all around the lake and we chased dragonflies, but they were too fast to catch."

"A new friend! Wonderful! I'm very happy for you," said The Tree. "And a waterfall! I cannot wait to hear all of your new stories."

As always, The Tree was very happy to learn about so many things which can't be seen from the hillside. Through the rest of the evening, Peep happily shared the stories of his adventure while The Tree listened intently and with true interest.

It was late into the night when Peep finally finished sharing his stories. Looking up at The Tree, he said with real honesty, "I really did like it by the lake, but it's good to be back home."

"I am happy you had such a wonderful adventure," said The Tree, "and I am glad that you are back in my branches."

Peep was quiet for a moment, then said thoughtfully, "I wish you could come with me to see all the new things I'm finding in the valley."

"I do, as well," said The Tree with true desire. "I think of you and your adventures often while you are away. But these are your adventures, my little bird. I am just happy you are willing to share the stories with me. I have been on this beautiful hillside for many years, but I have never before learned so much about the valley."

"I'm happy you're here to share them with," said Peep.

"Me, too," said The Tree.

They sat in silence for a long while until Peep finally settled himself down in the nest for the night. It had been a long day, so they said their 'goodnights' and quickly drifted off to sleep.

Looking Further

It was now well into autumn and a noticeable cold had begun to work its way a little deeper into each new day. The Tree had started to slow his growth to save energy for the coming long winter rest, and the fringes of his leaves had begun to turn gold and red.

Peep, however, was still eager for endless adventure. He flew deep into the valley nearly every day, spending most of his time away from his hillside home. The trips took him well past the lake and over and beyond the cliffs across the valley.

But most of Peep's time was spent at the open end of the forest, where the valley spread wide into open fields. He was looking toward the mountains in the distance, and would sometimes stay at the end of the valley for several days at a time.

The Mountains Beyond

Peep was out exploring again and The Tree was waiting patiently for his return. At last, Peep's homecoming call rang through the breeze, *Te-Tee!*, then he swooped under the coloring leaves and landed gracefully on the big branch.

"That was a good trip!" said Peep, not waiting for The Tree to ask the question.

"It is good to have you back!" said The Tree, "I thought about you often," as he said almost every time Peep returned.

Peep looked at The Tree and said rather seriously, "I went to the end of the valley again to look out at the mountains."

The Tree looked at him knowingly and said, "You have been there many times, looking to the mountains. It seems you might be ready for a very big adventure. Do you think?"

Peep was quiet and thoughtful for a little while, as if he had spent a long time debating his decision. He then said to The Tree with certainty, "Yes, my great friend, I am going to the mountains." Then after a short pause, he added, "Cheep said he will go with me, and we will need to leave soon to get there before winter settles in."

The Tree was quiet for another moment, then after a slow, deep breath, he smiled and said very softly, "I think it is where you are meant to go, my little bird. And I am glad you will have a friend with you to share the long journey."

Peep and The Tree looked at each other with just a little sadness in their eyes, then drifted into quiet thoughts of their own for a long time.

Finally, The Tree said very lovingly, "No matter how far from the valley you go, my little bird, I am here for you."

"I know you are, and I will always remember that," said Peep, feeling truly grateful for The Tree on the hillside.

Neither Peep nor The Tree were able to say much more to each other that evening. They both carried very strong emotions because they knew that once Peep left for the mountains, they would not see each other for a very, very long time. And, that Peep might even find and stay in a new home, far, far away from the valley.

Away

The Tree and Peep both woke up early for their last morning together. The sun had just begun to rise over the cliffs and the first rays of light touched the top leaves of The Tree.

The Tree quietly watched with pride as Peep skillfully glided through the branches and gathered up his breakfast. Peep very purposefully stayed within the leaves of The Tree to spend as much time as possible in The Tree's company.

The sun was now fully risen and Peep had waited as long as he could. He looked up at The Tree with sad eyes, wishing for more time, then took a long, slow breath and said, "I think it's time to go."

After a slight pause, and taking a slow, deep breath himself, The Tree gently echoed, "Yes, even after coming so far, you still have a very long journey ahead of you. I hope your adventure is everything you imagine."

"Thank you," said Peep. He then looked up through the branches and slowly hopped his way to the top of The Tree. When he reached the highest branch, he took a moment for a thoughtful look into the valley, just like the very first time he was on that branch.

The Tree knew his thoughts and said, "It was such a big valley the first time you saw it from up there. So many new adventures waiting for you."

"Hmm..." said Peep with a slight smile, "it doesn't look so big anymore." Then he looked toward the mountains and said more thoughtfully, "I guess my next adventures are beyond the valley."

Peep sat quietly for a moment more, then looked lovingly at The Tree and said, "In all my journeys and adventures, I will never find another tree who means as much to me as you."

The Tree had no words to answer, but stood up taller, feeling very thankful and grateful for Peep's love.

Then finally, Peep said with a very heavy voice, "Goodbye, my great friend, and thank you."

"Goodbye, my little bird," answered The Tree.

Peep turned toward the valley, took a short, deep breath for strength, and spread his wings. Letting go of the branch at the top of The Tree one last time, his home, Peep glided silently down the hillside and into the valley.

The Tree once again watched after Peep until long after he had faded into the distance. Eventually, he turned back to gaze across the wide valley, which suddenly seemed to feel very still and much quieter.

Despite his sadness, The Tree felt a new sense of gratefulness. He was thankful that Peep had come into his long life and had taught him so many new things about the valley, and that he had changed his life very much for the better.

The Tree took a deep breath and let out a long, slow sigh. Then, very quietly, he said, "And thank you, my little bird."

A Quiet Season

A few short weeks after Peep left for the mountains, the first light snow arrived in the valley, softening the rough texture of the forest. As the cold winter air settled in, the leaves of The Tree dried and dropped quickly, leaving only a few clinging to the very ends of his branches.

The Tree couldn't help but feel loneliness for the long, quiet winter ahead of him. But through the loneliness, the stories of Peep's adventures replayed in his mind and the valley looked slightly brighter to his eyes.

Eventually, The Tree drifted into a deep, lazy sleep that would last until the warmth of spring returned to revive him.

Waiting For Winter

The cold, quiet winter passed by slowly, until finally, the weather began to change. The thick blanket of snow took its time melting away, but eventually, treetops across the valley broke through the white to greet the new spring.

The sun brought its warmth to the hillside as well, and slowly woke The Tree from his long sleep. The snow quickly dripped away from his branches, and buds of new leaves began to poke their way through.

As he woke, The Tree's first thoughts were of hope for Peep's happiness in his new mountain home. He felt sadness for missing Peep, but still managed to gather up a faint smile, thinking how fortunate he was to at least have this wonderful view of the valley from high up on the hillside.

From his home above the valley, The Tree very much looked forward to seeing the forest green again and bustling with life.

An Unexpected Call

Now a few weeks into spring, The Tree's leaves had fully unfurled to soak up the warm rays of the sun. As The Tree gazed lazily across the valley, his thoughts often lingered on Peep, his adventures, and his new home in the mountains.

Calls from twittering birds floated up from the forest, reminding him of Peep's call when returning to the hillside. The Tree wondered if he would ever hear that call again, and in his daydreaming mind, he could almost hear Peep's call dancing lightly across the wind.

Then, quite unexpectedly, The Tree could swear that he actually did hear the call far in the distance. He straightened up a little and scanned over the treetops with a bit more focus. Then he heard it again, clearer and closer this time, *Te-Tee!*

The Tree was fully aware now. He looked intently toward the mountains, searching hard for a familiar sight among all the other birds crisscrossing through the air. Then again, *Te-Tee!* This time only a short distance away.

The Tree finally saw Peep just as he heard the last call. He watched with great surprise as Peep drew closer, then dipped down and swooped under his leaves. Too excited to even say hello, The Tree bristled with joy and simply smiled.

Peep landed gently on the big branch, as usual, but almost immediately after, another bird landed right next to him. It wasn't Cheep, so it appeared that Peep had made a new friend.

Peep Returns With Pip

"It is you, my little bird!" finally exclaimed The Tree.

"Ha... not so little anymore, my great friend," Peep said with a grin.

With much love and a light chuckle, The Tree answered softly, "Well... maybe not. But 'my little bird' you will always be to me."

They held each other's eyes for a long while, silently sharing the excitement and joy of being reunited.

Finally, The Tree said, "I see you have a new friend."

"Yes, I do!" said Peep very proudly. Then turning to the other bird, he added, "This is Pip, she is my mate!"

"Oh, I see! It is so very nice to meet you, Pip," said The Tree.

"Thank you! It's very good to meet you, too. I've heard an awful lot about you," said Pip. "And... I also call Peep 'my little bird' once in a while. I hope you don't mind."

"No, my dear, I do not mind at all," said The Tree with appreciation, "It means to me that you care for him as I do, which is a very good thing."

The Tree, Peep and Pip talked for a very long time that evening, sharing stories of the mountains and adventures beyond the valley. The Tree listened intently, grateful for the new stories, and grateful to hear Peep's voice again.

The Tree was far prouder and happier for Peep than he could possibly show on the outside. He was grateful that Peep had made it safely to the mountains, and especially that he had come back to visit the hillside once again. He was also very happy to see that Peep had found someone to love and care for, and who loved and cared for him just the same.

Finally, very late in the evening, The Tree said to Peep, "I am very happy you are here, my little bird. The mountains are so far away, and I was not sure if you would ever return to the valley. I have missed you very much." Then to Pip, he said, "And Pip, I am glad you are here with him."

Pip answered first, "Thank you very much. Peep told me so many wonderful stories of the valley and the hillside. I'm very happy to finally see it all."

Then Peep said to The Tree, "I have missed you too, my great friend, and I'm glad to be home."

The Tree raised an eyebrow and said, "Home? Did you not make a new home in the mountains?"

"Well, this has always been my home," said Peep softly.

Peep and Pip glanced at each other with a secretive smile, then looked back at The Tree. The Tree returned a curious look but was too exhausted to inquire any further.

It was well past dark and all three of them were very tired. So, after saying their 'goodnights', The Tree, Peep and Pip settled in, closed their eyes, and drifted off to sleep.

New Again

"Good morning!" said Pip, being the first to rise with the new sun.

"Good morning to you!" Peep answered with a tired voice.

The Tree heard their 'good mornings' through his sleep and slowly opened his eyes. "Good morning to you both," he said.

After a quiet moment, Peep said, "We talked very late into the night."

"Yes, we did!" said The Tree. "But I love hearing about your adventures. Your stories from the valley kept me happy through the long winter. Now I have many more to daydream about."

Then The Tree turned to Pip and said, "I think you will like our valley, Pip. You and Peep should explore as much of it as you can while you are here."

Pip and Peep glanced at each other again with another little smile.

The Tree saw the smiles, and said cautiously, "You... are planning to stay a while, are you not?"

Peep looked at The Tree and said, "Yes, I think we are. Like you said, there are lots of adventures in the valley to share with Pip," then glancing back at Pip, he added, "And maybe one or two new adventures for us to discover together."

"Well, that is good to hear!" said The Tree. "I am here for you, my little bird. And I am here for you, too, Pip."

"I appreciate that very much," Pip answered.

Peep's childhood nest did not survive the winter, but Peep showed Pip where it used to sit on the big branch. They whispered briefly between themselves, then Pip said to Peep, "It looks like we have a very busy day ahead of us."

Peep nodded in agreement, then looked at The Tree and said, "We would like to build a new nest here on the big branch. Would that be ok with you?"

The Tree was quite surprised at the question and fumbled out his words, "Yes... yes, that would be wonderful. I did not... Are you...?"

Peep and Pip smiled at The Tree with knowing looks in their eyes. Then Peep said, "We'll be back in just a bit." They then quickly flew off down the hillside as The Tree watched after them in wonder.

Just a few minutes later, Peep and Pip returned to The Tree. Their beaks were full of twigs and grass, and they immediately set themselves to building the new nest right where Peep's old nest used to sit.

The Tree was still in a bit of shock about what was happening and could only watch quietly as they set about their task.

They worked very hard through the day and into the night to finish the nest. The sides were built strong and high, and the bottom was filled with lots of soft grass and lost feathers from the valley floor. When they were finally done, they stood proudly on either side and admired their work.

"Well done to the both of you!" finally said The Tree, impressed with how well they worked together. "I think this is the nicest nest I have ever had in my branches."

"Thank you very much," they both said with true appreciation.

From the hard work through the day, Peep and Pip were very worn out and ready for a good night's sleep. The Tree would have loved to hear more stories, but he knew the tired couple needed their rest, so the three of them said their 'goodnights'.

What's This?

Peep quietly woke The Tree the next morning, just as the sun was rising over the cliffs, "Good morning, my great friend, we have something to show you."

With a sleepy voice, The Tree answered slowly, "Oh? What is it you have, my little bird?"

Peep then nodded to Pip, who gently stepped out of the nest. Resting snugly in the bottom lay three perfect little eggs.

The Tree's eyes grew wide with delight, and he said with great admiration, "Well... look what we have here. I had a feeling you two were up to something."

Pip and Peep gave The Tree a happy look of both playfulness and pride and said, "We wanted it to be a surprise."

"And what a surprise it is!" said The Tree. "Three beautiful little eggs!" The Tree's heart was overwhelmed with joy that another family would grow up in his branches.

To The Tree, Pip said, "Peep had so many wonderful stories about how well you took care of him and how much he loved the valley. So we decided to make our home and build our family here with you."

The Tree felt so grateful and humbled that he couldn't find any words to answer.

Peep then added, "I do like the mountains very much, but the hillside in the valley is my true home, and it always will be."

The Tree looked into their eyes and knew they understood what he was feeling. With three tiny new eggs in the nest, and Peep and Pip sharing his branches, there was nothing that could have made him any happier.

Time passed quickly over the next few busy weeks as Peep and Pip watched over the eggs. Pip stayed in the nest most of the time, keeping the eggs warm and well taken care of, while Peep busily gathered food for both Pip and himself.

The Tree put extra effort into growing thick with leaves to protect the nest from the wind, sun and rain, and to keep the family sheltered and safe in his branches.

Then, one calm and sunny day, The Tree noticed Pip and Peep standing at the side of the nest. They were looking intently at the three tiny eggs nestled inside. The Tree gazed curiously into the nest as well and noticed that every once in a while, the eggs wiggled just a little bit.

A crack had started on one of them and very soon after, a small piece of shell broke away and a tiny beak poked through. The shell chipped away a little more and a little more... until all at once, it split in two, and out came the first baby chick.

Both Pip and Peep took a deep breath and ruffled their feathers with joy.

The Tree said excitedly, but softly, "There is our first little one."

It didn't take long before the other two chicks had broken free of their shells as well.

Three brand new lives had come into the valley: a girl and two boys. They were tiny, their eyes were closed, and they had little stubs for feathers, but they were beautiful.

Pip and Peep gently removed the broken shells from the nest and fluffed up the bottom for their new babies. They looked thoughtfully at the chicks, whispered to each other, then said, "We will name you Pippi, Chip, and Tweets."

"Very good names!" said The Tree, feeling almost as proud as the parents.

Peep then climbed into the nest to keep the chicks warm and said to Pip, "I'll watch them for now. You go stretch your wings."

"Thank you," said Pip. "I'll gather some food for them as well." Then she turned and flew down to the forest.

The Tree and Peep sat quietly together, happy for the new little lives and for each other's company.

The Tree said thoughtfully to Peep, "It has been a long time since I first coaxed you out of your nest, my little bird, though I do remember it like it was yesterday."

"I remember, too," said Peep. "The whole world to me was inside these branches. I also remember the first time I looked across the valley from your highest branch. It was the first time I was outside the cover of your leaves, and the first time I knew that someday I would fly outside our home and far into the world."

The Tree nodded and added quietly, "And that is when I first saw the real wonder in your eyes and knew the true adventure in your heart. It was also the first time I understood just how much I would miss you while you were gone."

"I'm sorry," said Peep. "Back then, I hadn't thought of it that way, that you would miss me while I was away. I was thinking only of traveling across the valley and the adventures waiting for me."

"There is no need to be sorry. It is what I hoped you would want," said The Tree. "I could teach you only so much from up here on the hillside. I did my best to help you feel confident to reach out on your own."

"I thank you very much for that," said Peep with love. "You made me feel very safe inside your branches, so I also felt safe going outside. I was so eager to fly into the valley, to see as much as I could, just so I could come back and share it with you."

The Tree felt very happy and thankful for Peep's kind words, and said, "I am very proud of you."

In Good Hands

Time passed rather quickly over the next several weeks. The days and nights for Peep and Pip were busy with taking care of the chicks, gathering food, and keeping up the nest. Truly, it was all they had time to do. When one returned from gathering food, the other would immediately fly out to gather more.

Amidst the constant activity of them doing their work, The Tree watched patiently and contentedly.

The chicks opened their eyes a few days after they were born, but mostly they watched for their parents and the delivery of their next meal. When they weren't being fed, they gazed with curiosity into the branches and leaves overhead.

The chicks grew fast, and their feathers filled out to cover their bodies. They hadn't yet started talking, at least not much, but Peep and Pip began to teach them about The Tree and the valley.

Pippi, Chip, & Tweets

The Tree was happy to hear familiar words from when Peep first learned about his home. "All of this around you is The Tree. The Tree lives with you and you live with The Tree. The Tree shelters you from the wind and the rain, gives you shade from the sun, and protects you while you are young. The Tree will teach you and guide you as you grow. The Tree is your home in the valley."

Then, adding a few new words of his own, Peep said, "He is a good and kind Tree, and he will be here for you whenever you need him." Then glancing at The Tree with appreciation, he said, "He has always been here for me. He helped me to explore the valley with courage, and to find my way back home."

The Tree was thankful and humbled by Peep's kind words and could manage only a simple smile in return.

The curiosity of the young birds continued to grow. More and more, they looked around the branches and leaves of The Tree, studying their home and trying to understand what The Tree really was.

One sunny afternoon, the chicks were unusually quiet and huddled closely together in the nest. In turn, they each looked into and around The Tree, then whispered energetically between themselves. The Tree heard just enough to know that they were talking about him, and he guessed what they might be planning.

After a while, the chicks went very quiet and looked intensely at each other with both hope and uncertainty in their eyes. Finally, they looked up into The Tree, and with very nervous voices, squeaked shyly, "Hello?... Tree?" Then they quickly shrunk down into the nest, their eyes darting around in anticipation.

The Tree grinned slightly and waited an extra moment for dramatic effect, then he said in a soft and gentle voice, "Hello, my little birds. It is good to meet you."

The chicks stared wide-eyed at each other, then looked back up at The Tree and said, this time almost in unison, "It's good to meet you, too!"

Then, with much love, The Tree said to them, "I am here for you, my little birds."

Peep and Pip had been watching from the highest branch. They smiled down at the chicks, happy that they had finally reached out to The Tree.

Pip nodded to Peep, then flew into the valley. Peep stayed on the top branch a little longer. He watched as The Tree chatted happily with Pippi, Chip and Tweets. Peep thought fondly of his first day talking with The Tree and was very happy that his children would now learn from The Tree as he had.

The Tree glanced at Peep and they gave each other a soft smile of love and appreciation. The chicks were very eager, however, and had begun to ask another of a hundred questions they had saved up for The Tree, so The Tree looked back at them to give his full attention.

Peep lifted his head, let out a short, happy sigh and looked out over the valley as he had the first time he stood on The Tree's highest branch. *Our home on the hillside*, he thought warmly.

With one more look down at The Tree, he said very quietly, "Thank you for everything you have given me, my great friend."

Peep then turned back toward the wide, open valley and spread his wings.